Under the Terebinth

Under the Terebinth

Poems

Anna A. Friedrich

Foreword by Malcolm Guite

RESOURCE *Publications* • Eugene, Oregon

UNDER THE TEREBINTH
Poems

Copyright © 2024 Anna A. Friedrich. All rights reserved. Except for brief quotations in critical publications or reviews, no part of this book may be reproduced in any manner without prior written permission from the publisher. Write: Permissions, Wipf and Stock Publishers, 199 W. 8th Ave., Suite 3, Eugene, OR 97401.

Resource Publications
An Imprint of Wipf and Stock Publishers
199 W. 8th Ave., Suite 3
Eugene, OR 97401

www.wipfandstock.com

PAPERBACK ISBN: 979-8-3852-2845-4
HARDCOVER ISBN: 979-8-3852-2846-1
EBOOK ISBN: 979-8-3852-2847-8
VERSION NUMBER 09/12/24

For Dave,
the mighty oak under whose shade
I've long found shelter

Now the angel of the LORD came and sat under the terebinth...

and said to him, "The LORD is with you, O mighty man of valor." And Gideon said to him, "Please, my lord, if the LORD is with us, why then has all this happened to us? And where are all his wonderful deeds that our fathers recounted to us..."

JUDGES 6: 11–13 ESV

Contents

Foreword by Malcolm Guite | ix
Acknowledgments | xiii

Wings & Water

Imago | 3
A Lepidopterist Turns to Jazz to Make Sense of It All | 5
Every Night, a Funeral | 6
The Wild Yes | 7
Reservoir | 8
Pinioned | 9
Why do you seek the living among the dead? | 10
103 Esplanade | 12
Under the Terebinth | 13
Making a Home | 14
"I think we have that Oman song."—Dr. Salvatore Cerchio | 15
13 | 16

Liturgy

I. Anxiety/Coals | 19
II. Anxiety/Mud | 20
III. Anxiety/Waters of Baptism | 21
Ways You Went | 22
Something Understood | 23
Finally, a Poem about Boats and Storms and Jesus | 24
Kyrie | 25
Pseudacris crucifer | 27

Palm Sunday | 28
Good Friday | 29
Holy Saturday | 31
Easter Morning | 33

Beloveds

Fox | 37
A Painter and A Poet at the Science Museum, Boston | 39
For Silas, Advent 2020 | 40
lake garfield | 42
Memama | 43
For Barry | 44
Beloved | 45
Vespers | 49
Yours Is the Whale | 52
What Remains | 53

Sorrow

On Meeting Sorrow in the Woods | 59
Her Name Is Sorrow | 61
We the Bears | 63
Sorrow, nearly Fall | 64
Once, New, Sorrow | 66

Foreword

by Malcolm Guite

Poetry is a way of knowing, and the kind of knowledge it offers can be encountered in no other way. The poet takes the familiar, and, in Coleridge's phrase, removes 'the film of familiarity' so that we see things anew. 'Ordinary' things become vibrant, lucid, and sometimes, just sometimes, lucent with a light from beyond themselves. Then the images become symbols, lit from within by what Coleridge called 'the translucence of the eternal in and through the temporal'.

'In and through the *temporal*' is the important part of that phrase. Reason tends to fly away into abstraction, but the poetic imagination is concerned with the particular, the unique, the embodied, the incarnate. The more closely we look at the overlooked with the poet's eye, the more it has to offer us.

Anna Friedrich's fine first collection bears this out in many ways. The first poem, *Imago,* starts with attention to a tiny chrysalis, and all that might come from it if it lives, all that might be lost as it dies. The chrysalis is an image of the fragility of life but also the locus of inner life and hoped-for transformation, and almost every image in the poems that follow is in its own way a little chrysalis, an image from which a winged meaning is ready, if we will let it, to fly. That flight is the work of the poetic imagination, both the poet's and the readers', for as CS Lewis observed, 'Reason is the natural organ of truth, but Imagination is the organ of meaning'.

What these poems offer us is a way of reading the world, of reading the moment for its meaning, sometimes in the midst of the most difficult or desolate experience, as the poet says in her opening poem:

> like a chaplain whisked through a curtain
> and left in a hospital room, I try to read
> the moment, searching for signs of death
> while rehearsing my calling: hope.

And indeed, *hope* is the surprising thread or motif in a collection that deals unflinchingly with death, with loss, disappointment, diminishment, dementia. Like Gideon under the Terebinth, in the passage which gives this collection its title, the poet is searingly honest in asking the questions that suffering provokes:

Please, my lord, if the LORD is with us, why then has all this happened to us? And where are all his wonderful deeds that our fathers recounted to us..."

And yet the hope that comes in this collection, the hope which the poet offers as her *calling*, comes not in the form of certain answers to the questions we ask under the Terebinth, but comes rather in a growing intuition of that tenacious love that sustains us even as we question it. The love that somehow deepens in the face of death, the love that also holds at least the hint and hope of resurrection. Indeed, those hints and hopes, offered in the first part of the collection, 'Water and Wings' are what sustain us in the later poetic sequences on anxiety and sorrow. So image after image in that section suggest a coming transformation:

> But this caterpillar
>
> seems ecstatic
>
> in her flailing,
>
> final molt. She hangs
>
> headfirst; she dives
>
> into the grave
>
> chrysalis dark,
>
> as if somehow
>
> she heard Jesus say
>
> *Why are you weeping?*
>
> *She is only*
>
> *asleep.*

The Biblical allusion there is one of the rare direct citations, for this collection has a rich and complex relation with both scripture and liturgy. It could not be further away from some work of shallow devotion festooned with proof texts, all on the surface. On the contrary we sense in many of these poems a long, subtle, sometimes oblique conversation with the stories of scripture and the seasons of the liturgical year, a conversation that happens not on the glossy surface, but in the 'inky depths.' As Friedrich says in *Something Understood*, a poem which is also in conversation with George Herbert's poem *Prayer*, from which its title comes:

> Something crept towards me
> halfway through the church service.
> I think it was a prayer—
> I felt its eye on me, unblinking and rather
> than approaching from the nave
> or the altar, it came from some
> inky depths where I believe
> darkness is meant to have been lit
> right out of existence.

The kind of faith that is on offer in this collection is not a series of proclamations but rather a wrestle with the angel, a wrestle that is sometimes a dance. And that of course is what poetry does best: Wrestling and Dancing.

Acknowledgments

Many thanks to the editors of these journals, magazines, chapbooks, TV programs, and conference directors where the following poems first appeared, sometimes in earlier versions:

Art on the Trails: Marking Territory: "On Meeting Sorrow in the Woods"

Common Good: "lake garfield," "Finally, a Poem about Boats and Storms and Jesus"

CRUX: "Every Night a Funeral," "Yours is the Whale"

EcoTheo Collective: "A Painter and A Poet at the Science Museum, Boston"

Fare Forward: "Imago"

The Rabbit Room online: "Reservoir"

The Rabbit Room's Poetry Substack: "Memama," "Ways You Went," "Vespers"

Three Things Newsletter: "For Barry" (under the title "Victory, indeed"), "Easter Morning" (under the title "Good talk, good talk")

"Her Name Is Sorrow" was commissioned by contemporary classical composer Anselm McDonnell for his album *Kraina*, sung by tenor Joshua Ellicott

"Imago," "A Lepidopterist Turns to Jazz to Make Sense of It All" (under the title "Jitterbug"), "Every Night, a Funeral," "The Wild Yes," "Holy Saturday," "A Painter and A Poet at the Science Museum, Boston" were all included in The Butterfly Project, a two-year (and seemingly, wonderfully, unending!) body of work with visual artist Heidy Sumei Chuang, in collaboration with the Christian environmental conservation group A Rocha

"Imago," "Every Night, a Funeral," "The Wild Yes," "*Ways You Went*," "Holy Saturday," "On Meeting Sorrow in the Woods," were all featured on a local TV show, Wake Up and Smell the Poetry, thanks to Cheryl Perreault

"*Why do you seek the living among the dead?*" was included in Housemoot 2024 by the Rabbit Room

"II. Anxiety/Mud," "III. Anxiety/Waters of Baptism" were included in the Easter Vigil at Church of the Cross in Boston

All Bible quotations from the ESV

Wings & Water

Imago

On the back porch
in late summer I sit stunned
beside my son Adam.

The porch is a hundred years old
with new boards freshly
painted sky blue.

Adam is eleven: lanky and curious, crouching
next to me like a monkey—*mon petit singe*—
but motionless.

Our first caterpillar chrysalis turned black
last night, and we are nearly crying.

What was a jade green bulb
with a golden crown
that we protected, propped
up, prayed for—shrouded
this morning: a lump of coal
on a broken branch.

Is it dead?
he asks.

Like a chaplain whisked through a curtain
and left in a hospital room, I try to read
the moment, searching for signs of
death while rehearsing
my calling: hope.

Let's wait and see
I answer.

And that is enough for him

to dash into the day
unencumbered.

A month ago, he dubbed
this caterpillar *Lucky*
and like the first Adam
he has a knack for naming.

A Lepidopterist Turns to Jazz to Make Sense of It All

When she falls
   into adulthood
      suspense makes room
for wings, silent pulsing
   fills the measure
     of her veins
       watch—
         the tempo change

When she rises
   nearly ready—
     slow crawl
into the spotlight,
   sunshine strikes
      her scales, plays a
        movement unsung
       in her old skin

When she falls
   into a trumpet bloom
     to tongue
that first sweet tune, ah!
   coiled longing
      springs, fulfilled—
       her body
       hums

When she rises,
   rich, unruly—
     to dance
along the highway,
   her wingbeats
      clap revival only
        God
        can hear

Every Night, a Funeral

Every night, a funeral

rehearsal in my bed. I lie

again, after a mere day

given to reclaim

conscious thought—

voice—

loves—

Then the awful

necessity of sleep

takes hold.

But this caterpillar

seems ecstatic

in her flailing,

final molt. She hangs

headfirst; she dives

into the grave

chrysalis dark,

as if somehow

she heard Jesus say

Why are you weeping?

She is only

asleep.

The Wild Yes

Her grave clothes

    tear and seem to shrink

        into paper so thin, I reach

    out to catch her but she clings—

like Ruth to Naomi, her strength is

        young but sure. I hold, instead, my breath.

    Antennae flicking—if she could blink

        she would be blinking—her old dusty

            frame now like a freshened leaf, in

                spring. If you are so lucky

            as to see her first full extension

                the flutter

                in your own belly

        will match the wild *yes*

    that the butterfly

        knows.

Reservoir

The swans have mated
again, despite the virus—
seven cygnets, fuzzy, golden
huddle in the reservoir
between their cob and pen.
Each in turn dives, apprenticed in
the slow current. Crickets
chirp along the banks
though it's almost midday.
Poison ivy sprouts
across Beale's path and
pollen from white pines dusts
the water's surface and its debris,
dusts my skin, dusts everything
because this is the season
of determination—
when winter's layers
peel back like a mask
and hope in every species
flings wide as if irrevocable.
I let their voices accompany
the call of the mourning dove
into my inner ear—
the labyrinth where I've
heard, equilibrium
resides.

Pinioned

I'm trying to make sense of the swan
on the highway—how I swerved
to miss it, and missed my exit—

how the truck, three cars back, didn't budge,
barreling down the center lane. Not a pair

of swans, just one. All white, unearthly, why
did she step, and step again, onto I-93 one fall
afternoon?

I saw her neck
stretched high, agitated, maybe
searching for a way

through the maze
of incalculable machines. The noise

did not finally deter her—I don't know
if swans see color but she seemed to safely
dodge a bright red sedan.

I swerved, as I've said, not *unto death*
but dangerously. Recovering, chilled,
I could not help

but watch in my rear-view mirror—
O she extended to full measure, almost angelic
as if to fly. But that truck clipped

her right wing, pure-feathered, and
sent her spinning.

Why do you seek the living among the dead?

No ocean I know
resounds in the dusting spiral
of a whelk—I've sounded

them for decades
caught in the surf
after only a glimpse

in darkness I've grasped
towards the thing
risked

a full-bodied knockdown
in the ebb just to reach it

and oh! sometimes a crab
or discarded concrete—

I snatch it quick
like a child elated
or it pinches me, defying
my grip—either way

I'm shouting when I emerge, reckless
against the rolling tide.

If a whelk, I'm Aladdin
with treasure in hand
tossed and beaten

by endless waves, after being
sloughed off. It's tempting

to forget once it was home
to a slow sea snail—

armored, she muscled
her rippling way through
our rhythmic world. Only lore

tells of cadence deep hidden
in calcium carbonate—
it's not my blood

pulsing in time, echoing back
in her empty shell, no

the rising swell I hear
can't be my own.

103 Esplanade

for Kimberly

Two eagles play
by the river—let's not
reduce it

to a mating ritual.
Or let's—as creatures
without conscience
without surety
their aim

is simple:
to go on.

But if their game
is more birdlike
than you or I imagined—

all rise and risk, real
chatter, composition, song—

riding secret currents, warm
with readied eye and honed—

> *Let joy back in* (I think
> I hear you say)

> *Two eagles play*
> *by the river.*

Under the Terebinth

Here I come
at hope
from a wide angle—

like I'm drunk and not
agreeing with gravity—

like an eagle unbeckoned
perches on my right arm,

his varied lids
slide up and over one
eyeball at a time—is he

looking at me? I am
no tamer—

> *Let feather upon*
> *feathers, dense—denser*
> *than sand packed together*
>
> *guide my upward glance,*
> *a sky-born promise*
> *given*
>
> *in vision, between*
> *blinks.*

Making a Home

Making a home, you need

flowers and dirt,
glass and plastic, stone,
fabric, maybe feathers

depending on who you are
(if a bird, you'll need feathers for sure)

but I only use them decoratively
even superfluously, some
might say—

they don't add warmth
except the soul kind—the kind
that says I was waiting for you,
squinting out the front window,

fluffing pillows, stacking clean plates
to put away warm, readied. I even

bought a spare toothbrush
because who knows—

we all forget, when in a
rush, or on the run, and breath

is such an intimate thing—

coming from down inside
you, where it's nearly
one hundred degrees, but

without tending, it reeks.

"*I think we have that Oman song.*"
—Dr. Salvatore Cerchio

My instruments, off the coast of Oman
picked up a whale song—

two notes never heard
quite like this   *da . . . dum*

So low, so slow their song—
my instruments sped it up twenty times
for the human ear
to be able to hear new

blue whales off the coast of Oman.

A thousand feet down
da . . . dum
the instruments found
a population
            —how many?

Each a hundred feet long,
each tongue weighs two tons
            (and then some)

singing *da . . . dum* deep in the sea
off the coast of Oman.

The largest animal
ever known—a *population*

we missed and now this—a new song!
Out of the depths, surprised

to detect *da . . . dum*
whereas three or four is the norm—

just two notes in the dark—
Oman song.

13

Every thirteen seconds
a foghorn sounds, filling this blue sky
morning in June.

Maine's northern shore signals
a warning with one single note

*Beware! Granite islands abound
along this drowned coast
harboring countless evergreens...*

Sitting on a whale rock already
half-submerged
as the tide inches in, I count

the seconds between each
needless blare: thirteen.

It's a low G note, I'm convinced
after three days of listening, wandering
the octave. I came by car

to a downeast isle
expecting silence, not this

urgent rhythm all day long, all
night, too. They say a sensor's

broken in the relentless horn—
a lighthouse of sound, not guiding
anyone, except to distraction.

Just shut the whole thing down I want to cry
out in the night. Thirteen seconds pass—

I'm reminded again, here at the sea
things get iffy quickly and people
are prone to get lost.

Liturgy

I. Anxiety/Coals

Just when will I get to
Elijah-level desolation?

Must there be
suicide, an irreversible
move, a maniacal
woman, or will run-of-the-mill

betrayal do the trick? Basically
Lord, I'm asking
when to expect

ravens
by the brook?

How long before you, O
Mighty One, bring me

bread, yourself

—prepared your favorite
way (over hot coals)
or meat—

Send out the birds,
the angels, all the wings
of heaven—anything

that swoops
down to accompany
the Voice

> *Get up and eat,*
> *the journey*
> *is too much*
> *for you*

II. Anxiety/Mud

I sat down to work
and there's dirt

on my table, dirt
in my hair don't even
ask about my fingernails—

I've been digging
in a cave, all day, as prophets

do—just a child
wild for jewels, whining,
hungry, tugging
at a hem I trust

responds. Mud
in pie plates
packed and smooth

looks like chocolate—
every white stone
a pearl, Lord

I'm filthy, I know
but I sold
everything, I've lost

my life. The cave is still
dark—call my name,

remember?
You promised

a holiday
at the sea.

III. Anxiety/Waters of Baptism

Ease this busy mind, Lord—

    the worry wandering, daily

        paths of perfect peacelessness—

    wade in with me

           and wend through ways

that wind relentlessly.

We beseech thee—light the ancient, darkened pass

    I'm weary of risking alone—flooded,

    footsore, ever on the edge

of frantic—*Where is your faith?*   you ask

    as if the storm were a sprinkle, as if

the fury were imagined? It's night

Lord, thrashing waves require an

        attentiveness   I fear

    you do not offer—

    vigilant, I groan, I grasp, and circling

without you, drown.

Ways You Went

I wake up in a crowded room.

Dreams that worked my jaw all night
press in then dissipate. Alone, I turn to see
my husband is already up, the kettle proves
he knows I love hot coffee when

I wake. Up in a crowded room
in heaven, that cloud of witnesses
turns to see me rise into
a new day—bra, skirt, sweater,
shoes, keys, guilt that pokes
and nags and wonders why

I wake up. In the crowded room
behind my eyes spreadsheets spread
while I drive, demanding—
Total the lattes this year.
Add the cost of the sweater against
the hunger and injustice in your

wake. Up in a crowded room
in the city, elected men address
their lists and calendars—power
calls to power, maneuvering
in the graceless dark that you and

I wake up in. A crowded room
is no place to ask *Where is God?*

But go ahead.

Something Understood

Something crept towards me
halfway through the church service.
I think it was a prayer—
I felt its eye on me, unblinking and rather
than approaching from the nave
or the altar, it came from some
inky depths where I believe
darkness is meant to have been lit
right out of existence. Who's to say
and does its derivation matter—hell
I don't know. Why
it was shrouded in a prayer
seems like a question for Rothko
or Hopkins—all was bleared, smeared
on the second row in the sanctuary
as the people knelt

> *Lord in your mercy hear*
> *our prayer.*

Finally, a Poem about Boats and Storms and Jesus

I've tried to write it
before, but I get sucked out
and flipped around with every tide—
the rip current of the Apostles'
Creed wrests me way off
shore where any vessel I know
to clamber onto is full
of men with little faith—

I end up in the bow
without fail, frantic
for a pillow, believing that if
someone could just fall asleep (not me)
—find that much rest inside himself—
we might, I don't know, catch 153
fish, or walk on water, maybe see
a ghost. I tend to beg

to be thrown overboard
but no one's drawing straws;
they're not afraid. And I am
not their prophet. So I roam
the open sea on every page.

Kyrie

Racing on the elliptical
against a digital timer
and a faux incline,

I consider my death.

A red heart flashes
while it finds
my heart rate—the number

offers me a small comfort
or rebuke.

I push and pull
like this work matters, till sweat
drops. I haven't gone anywhere.

Gregorian chants in my
cheap earbuds, discordant

alongside the pulsing
dance-pop that fills Planet
Fitness, late Ash Wednesday.

Six empty contraptions
on either side of me—
gasping, alone; I'm thirsty.

And writing poems? Ridiculous
at this pace. I see

the ashes

that mark me
in the blank TV screen
propped up before my face. The dust

has sunk into every forehead
crease, Lord

have mercy. My machine
counts down—3, 2, 1—

Pseudacris crucifer

With swelling throats, as if to burst,
peepers at our pond's edge

lift their heads
a thousand strong.

It's just a mating call—
not a curse on winter's work,
not quite hosanna, to bless
the coming spring. We don't know

how they know the days
are lengthening.

Their given name, *Cross-bearer,*
for the mark on each wet back—

year after year, relentless,

in Lent they bear their cross
—*I'm here*
they scream, *for this I came!*

Even at dusk, where hope
could fade—the chorus

frogs sing,
I'm here! I'm here!

Palm Sunday

Over lunch, a conflagration

of car horns, a woman
with her white megaphone,
and a high school marching band—

humans—loud, impassioned, fill
the Common in downtown Boston.

Simba's *I Just Can't Wait to Be King*
blends with chants on Park Street, a wildfire
of noise turns the corner—"genocide"
the only word I catch.

Is it the sun—a surprise

mid-March—that lit these souls, gathered
at the fountain, on the grass,
and every sidewalk? Light like this

on the outer edges
of winter, sparks. So I join
the procession, restless

to wander, to dance, to shout

at pedestrians who disobey
the signs, walking
with a sense

of their own courage
to an unknown destination.

Good Friday

The wind keeps me
from my walk today.
To wrap up

in my scarf, without feeling
a noose around my neck—

to tuck in my shirt securely—
to pull my socks up over the hem
of my pants

so I won't be forced
to do it twice—it's all too much.

I want to move
       my body

out into the world save
the question
of things unraveling.

              The wind

wraps around our flat
like a whip—
like a dragon's tail.
Pausing in the stairwell,
I check the elm

—try to measure
its bend and weight against
my son's corner bedroom.

              The wind

—as if to peel
back the crust of the earth

sends dust, candy wrappers, a shoe
whirling—makes us huddle
in our homes, not taking walks

—*Dammit*
       a sudden wallop

then a slow persisting drone—it's not
a dance I know.

I pause my hurried steps
again on the landing,
a load of dirty clothes
resting at my hip—the next

gust—calculating, I can only

watch the pale porch curtains
wrangle, spill,
twist, and fly.

Holy Saturday

      I apologize
for the metaphor, dear
Caterpillar. I've read you

like a Bible verse that caught
my eye, scrawled on a city bench
far from home. The wily human

heart longs for something purer
than luck or chance—
            uncontaminated

hope. I've watched you
grovel on what they call
(I kid you not) *false legs*

and how you eat and eat
beyond appetite—it's all
too familiar, Caterpillar.

How you one day
turn in, get awfully quiet

wound up and bound
to a secrecy, I see you there—

no fresh air, no sunlight.
You must question
the royal title
in the darkness, *Monarch*.

      So yes, you bring to mind
the old Pharaohs mummified, and Jesus
wrapped up in strips of linen

altogether still, and my own baby
swaddled, in a shoe box, buried

under the purple butterfly
bush in bloom.

Easter Morning

it all started with
Adam's fried egg slipping
off his plate and into the open
silverware drawer—we were
already late—steaming
orangey goo covered every clean
sharp knife so I yelled

hallelujah!—held breath released, all clenched

teeth slackened, raised eyebrows fell
back into position then the laughter
came, shook the kitchen, racked our bodies
and settled down into hugs all
around it's ok it's all
going to be ok

Beloveds

Fox

Reading Hölderlin
      puts me in a mind
to abandon poetry
altogether. So in defiance
with my coffee and a cookie, I open

Mary O to remember
the fox, his teeth
my teeth
our throats—

the only place a poem
can breathe. *Someday we'll live
in the sky* she writes, surely
doubting. Not you too

Mary—flying off
to heavenlies devoid and fixed
while Hölderlin mocks on,

      Narrow domesticity!
      You and your *glebae addicti—*

that's how I read him. That's how
I read the fox gleaming, tooth and eye.
That's how I gladly drink this cup
of burnt beans.

Toby, on the Common
with one eye lost, tells me
my dog looks like a fox.

Every morning another stranger
stops to say the same—a fox
on my leash, tamed (hardly).

She eats every stray bit God
knows I try to lead her

away from. She domineers
any creature we encounter—
it's embarrassing.

She is blind.

And her teeth, startling still, less
white at fifteen, yet she seems
to know she could use them—

       if threatened, she must.

A Painter and A Poet at the Science Museum, Boston

for Heidy Sumei Chuang

Watching   butterflies   with Heidy

     a slow and quiet craft—   pages open, tell a story

too short   then close.

     Mystery befriends the patient.   No one knows

this   better than the butterfly (or painter)—July

     is full of heat and hunger,   here   she learned to worm

to fly   into her life from strength to strength

     only weeks wide and wild. With one brush   she livens

symmetry   and surprise   before we catch each other's eye.

     A glint on the Charles   bids her rise

                 and flutter by.

For Silas, Advent 2020

"*About midnight Paul and Silas were praying and singing hymns to God. . ."* Acts 16:25

Remember, months ago

we feared we'd never meet you

alive. The midwives, whose only task—

to welcome and make room—instead

delivered other news: all was not well.

All was not well inside of you.

Another thing had grown, a mass,

in your right lung, threatening

that breath you first must take—

already robbed? Ours, too

choking on a possibility—never

knowing you beyond a flutter (that secret

hope of every mother, fragile

as a fresh-winged butterfly) but now

Praise be, your second advent—

not from the womb,

but from the surgeon's table

where scalpel scarred your so-young skin,

freed you from darkness, *Silas!*

Like your namesake,

the prison doors have opened

you are free—to breathe the air

to pray and sing your hymns

as we sing ours, for you.

lake garfield

compare and compete, compare and compete

I can hear them bicker from the shore

my boys are out fishing

in a borrowed canoe

while the sun seems

to fill the lake till it breaks

out in ripples their

chests and arms gleam

as they cast, reel in, re-cast

we've caught nearly thirty fish they holler

together, I wave, they shout back

all catch and release—

catch and release the younger repeats

as if it's a song

the line in his hand flung, flies

laughter rolls in to the dock

echoes back catch

and release

Memama

Who wants to hear of hospice, incontinence,
the rags and ruined carpets—

especially when it's your mother
in that bed, whose creaks
and metal railings make the farmhouse den
more of an institution.

The TV's on, has been since you remember;
the piano quiet for fifty years, more?
Mom is gentle now, strains to a smile
but asks about the good Lord's will in all of this.

Silent, your eyes lift, rest on the handwritten
family tree, still crooked on the wall
next to Dad's taxidermied turkey.

One room over, in the blue
recliner all but blind, he grunts
with (let's say) gratitude
as you hoist the one who nursed you
nearly seventy years ago.

You chat through the shuffle to the bathroom
as if you'd always embraced like this.

She needs you in the night now,
so you're sleeping in your childhood
bedroom, where a blue-eyed Jesus
looks down. He's knocking

at the door—
you know the one.

For Barry

The morning, still dark

could not shed light on us

when Dave tells me

your cancer has spread.

I am stretched out

across the turquoise couch

after a hard night, contending

with my own disease. My legs

are cold—a few days' bristles

snag at the hem

of an insufficient robe.

Scanning the room in need

of a blanket, but Dave keeps

talking, so

I tuck my legs up under

the weight of my own body

shiver and go on

searching his sentences, his pauses

for a prayer we cannot

articulate.

Beloved

Marriage is lived
in the bathroom at least
at our house—
the waiting, pains and pushing,
anticipatory leg-shaving
pungent exchanges in the morning
nose hair trimmings (not my own)
and toothpaste glumps (also not mine)

the angry clorox wiping
and fingernails—
freaking fingernails strewn
everywhere, how can so few make it

into the wastebasket?
It's all about the body,
being married—two bodies, O
I mean more than
communing in the dark

I mean looking for the faint
blue line a couple
dozen times together, me on the toilet
you by the sink, yes
toilet paper has many uses—
I mean the swell and ache and moan
of new life, I mean
our squirmy baby boy in an inch of warm
water, I mean get the magic

eraser, please, I mean
who will clean
the tub this time
and maybe we should
re-caulk, I mean the bandaids and
the scales of marriage, the night light

and the soap of marriage, I mean essential
oil poured out, overtaking, I mean hunting
for pimples, plucking undesirables—

I don't bother with makeup, but it's
in the mirror I see

we are not what we were, bemoaning
as we slide the curtain aside
cleaning drains, clipping bangs, noting gray
growing. We meet on the floor
where one is crying—

we're on hands and knees
scooping up our nephew's vomit,
wide-flung kitty litter,
finding drops of blood, lost.

People say a lot about the heart
when it comes to marriage
and true enough
my chest pounds,
it hurts, at times
it grows, O dear—
like the Grinch, responding

to you, Dave,
        your immeasurable kindness.

Yes, my heart is surely involved
but marriage is more skin
and hair—these are not our favorite
things, the spots, the change

we keep meeting
in a rush

on the cold stone floor, in what you call
the washroom, our hearth—

just a soft yellow box
of a room, damp space,
on the second floor
where we are

sleepless
jealous
mean
sick
cleaned
undone
afraid
gentle
embarrassed
ourselves
beloved—

        I saw Memama reach for Grandaddy's hand
        the coloring was all wrong though
        everyone said he looked so natural
        she talked to him, like a crazy person

        walking down the center aisle of the funeral home
        stumbling, really, toward the open
        casket, telling him about the flowers
        that surrounded him that's when
        she grabbed his hand

        stiff, blue-veined—
        it must be a core memory of mine, the two
        of them dancing

        how they'd go quiet, Memama folding
        into Grandaddy's tempo—known, fluid
        no one else could follow his lead

        they grinned, unaware
        of all but hands and hips

the music

—ok Love, it's getting late,
let's dance.

Vespers

What a waste—

when you had a poem
to write, but instead you were robbed

of one whole writing
day—because your
kitten escaped—

found an evergreen
a block away

right after you
trimmed her claws—

turns out ascension's
easier than

coming down—she
meowed, Meowed until

neighbor Irene
came out in the cold

cursing me,
her dead husband,
the town—

she meowed and
meowed, frozen,
out on a limb

too high
for the fire department
(I called them)—40 feet?

A liability—
there's no risking life

or limb of a brave
civil servant

for a 4-month-old
kitten. So I prayed, at least
seven times, I invoked

the name of the One Who
Came Down.

While I stood
in fresh snow,
What a waste
I repeated—

gazing upwards
for hours
until my neck cramped—

until hungry, muddied
beyond what you'd think,

dragging logs, forgotten
siding, an abandoned red slide,
anything—

ever hoping
for an unlikely turn. By-God

I found
an old, broken ladder
under ice and leaf litter—

my husband, a once-
upon-a-time-firefighter,

biked home from the office,
put on his ski helmet

(Irene paced
and warned)

—my beloved climbed up
that rickety thing,

reached for and secured
our small, precious one,
the one we named

Vesper, she's the color
of night, she's

ignorant, ambitious,
afraid—

like a poet.

Yours Is the Whale

a lament for Miranda Harris

O God of wallet-findings—
God of ibis and of ocean—
God of continental drift, butterflies,
    and landfills—
God of all volcanoes, rascals, lilies,
    and the mounding mums outside the coffee shop—
God of the maple tree, every tsunami—
    wild rabbit in our field—
    salamanders in the creek—
O God of snapping tendons—
God of the U.S. Senate—
God of loss and climate, changed—Yours is the whale, Lord,
    Yours, too, the virus.
God of walking trails, oil rigs, arresting officers—
    victim and perpetrator both look to you, O God
    beyond the moon—
God who wrestles men beside the River Jordan—

O God of brimming wedding wine, my husband
    lost his wallet on his birthday!
        I cried out to you
    for mercy; it appeared. Dear
Miranda's car plummeted from the bridge
    at that same hour.

What Remains

for Peter

His nose drips incessantly
now, he's unable
to wipe it—
he's losing speech—
cannot stand—
is afraid of the lift
that helps him
into the washroom—
looks to a stuffed
animal for little comfort—
he's losing teeth
as quickly as memories—
his left side, paralyzed—
his right, not
far behind—
he doesn't know me
anymore, *I am crying*
he often says as he
begins to cry

at the mention of an unforgettable
bike ride in his youth,
Fiddler on the Roof,
a former pastor, or the choirs
he loved—then he begins
in German, long drawn-out phrases—

we don't understand.

His son wipes his eyes,
his chin, and then, as if resurrected
this white-haired man, with the clarity
of a soloist belts out

> *Then sings my soul, my Savior, God, to Thee*
> *How great Thou art! How great Thou art!*

We've joined in, ready to repeat the lines
but he stops, slides back into mumbling—
twitching uncontrollably—
his wheelchair squeaks.

We are silent awhile, then he manages
to read his grandson's sweatshirt
with his high school logo,
Boston Trinity

Is it a Christian school?
Yes, Grandpa
Are you a Christian?
Yes, Grandpa, I am

I'm proud of you, he says in all earnestness,
and he awakens again
with the voice of a young man

> *I have decided to follow Jesus*
> *I have decided to follow Jesus*
> *I have decided to follow Jesus*
> *No turning back, no turning back*

We all join in,

> *Though none go with me, still I will follow*
> *Though none go with me, still I will follow*
> *Though none go with me, still I will follow*
> *No turning back, no turning back*

He stops and looks at us, emptied,
then, asks about a picture
on his shelf, always the same one—

his grandchildren. The frame does more
than just hold a picture, it is
battery-operated, and hidden in it,
the treasure of four of his eight
grandchildren's voices, recorded,

each offering
a favorite Grandpa saying—

The bus is leaving!
Yabbi dabbi doo!
Grandpa's noodles!
Oh goodness sakes!

and then together they sing
We love you Grandpa!

He breaks into a smile, repeats
to himself, *We love you Grandpa. . .*

He looks around the room
confused. None of those four
are here at this moment.

These are your grandsons, too
Peter, the ones from Boston!

Boston, he repeats
Boston, then nearly shouts

    The cross before me, the world behind me

We join him,

    The cross before me, the world behind me
    The cross before me, the world behind me
    No turning back, no turning back

It's time to go

but when we wheel him out,
weaving through a dozen
occupied wheelchairs facing
a blank TV,

all the way to the fake
Christmas tree, decorated
in haste with cheap ornaments
he cries out in his perfect baritone

    O Tannenbaum! O Tannenbaum!

then chuckles, as if to himself—
and in the momentary light of lucidity
he smiles at that tree, smiles
up at us and declares

with perfect ease,
Man, I've got it good.

Sorrow

On Meeting Sorrow in the Woods

she said
tears can score a tree

I couldn't possibly agree
I said
*think of the years of rings and weathering
how storms have pummeled trees with rain
yet they remain*

she said
*my tears come from my god
the god of Grief who ever cries
without relief*

*I know gods
don't cry like that*
I sighed and sat

beside her on the path, where
she greeted fireflies—there were
seashells in her hair

she lifted leaf litter
like a child in her arms

she said
*my tears always start, not in my heart
but in my toes*

I looked down then—
her feet were bare but caked with mud

she said
*my tears are bigger
than any you've seen before*

on my own cheeks? I asked
the ones that splashed my infant's grave?

she turned away, to catch her breath
I guess—when she returned, she gave me

one tear, from her own eye:

boulder-sized, I could not hold it
not with ropes or measuring cups

its will and weight fell
and washed me clean—

after the storm

I searched for her
to tell her *I believe*

Her Name Is Sorrow

Thank you she said
it like a question
while we walked along
ocean, creek, tributary

-made no difference-

our conversation was all
chemistry—alkali
and acid: elemental sisters warring,
waiting—we, their mediators.

Taking my hand, she made me
hold the life gone from a starfish, then took

my arm and led me to Jennette's pier, now decrepit?
She took my eyes and told me I'd be fine

in heaven blind—she took my eyes!—
one in each enormous hand

and chucked them in the sea so I might
see the coral reef's white bones
she mused

then left me shouting on the beachrock
like Bartimaeus.

My eyeballs floated
in the flotsam before one sank
in the drink; it must have been
my weightier eye—serious, tireless, landing
long after in a bathyal baleen
whale fall.

The other—my light-hearted eye
rushed into a shallow current
rich with a community
of pink and purple plastic.

Above the sea, the rest of me sat down
in defeat. Soaked by unexpected waves
—not tears, my eyes were lost, recall—I cried
out with the seagulls

Sorrow! Sorrow!
until I sensed her presence—

mercy, shame...again
she said *Thank you*—her voice
wide and deep inside a yawn. The tide
came up to tuck her in

to bring the night's oblivion
which makes the day's woes

bearable—its acid
and its alkaline—she slept,
I think. And I awoke.

We the Bears

Sorrow dreamt of reckless
bears who overate, who
clawed more trees
than could recover.

The sharper grew
a she-bear's claws the more
devoted she became
to salmon breakfast,
lunch, and dinner. Hunger
beyond nature ruled, consumption

was her Rule of Life. She even gave
up sleeping when she learned
that hibernation kept her
quiet for a season. A minimizing
of her presence? Queen-Bear rebuffed—
declared rest
shameful.

Unflinching, enormous, ever
fiercer, she rallied bears
for winter-wading in the river

while newborn cubs
neglected, froze. Who
led the march of wide-eyed bears
to open sea—

where waves,
more careless
overcame them, swallowed up
those reckless bears?
Sorrow rolled
and dreamt again.

Sorrow, nearly Fall

I was weeding two raised beds

when she arrived,

tugging bindweed between rows

of mounded potatoes. The work

was quick, my hands aware of where

to dig, which rooted treasures

must be left a little while longer.

The ground

was late-summer-cracked-and-dry,

a little *puff* of dust released

each time I snapped a rhizome—

Angry, I admit, at poorly

named Morning Glory—still, Sorrow watched

me, stooped and curious, held out

her hands (as wide as wheelbarrows),

to catch the weeds I threw

towards a heap.

—*Yes?* I asked

—*This is violence,* Sorrow whispered, *Puff!* I chucked

another; she caught it tenderly, wound

it up like Christmas ribbon

—*No, this is life on earth,* I said, *Growing,*

growing, some intended, some perverse

—*You decide,* Sorrow scoffed, *which green*

goes on? Are you the one to choose?

—*I am.* My violence

turned to sport, throwing noxious

vines as far or wide as I was able—

she ran

so not one fell, forgotten,

unattended.

Once, New, Sorrow

She lands in the front lawn
like a white, foaming sea wave—

earnest, uninvited. She overtakes
the porch, as if humidity herself.
The porch is my chest

where she sits heavy

on a creaking
rocking chair. Each movement strains
the wooden joints; the rhythm

she begins is anything
but comforting.

Hydrangeas line the drive, or did
before she crushed

half of the blueish clusters, too much
for brittle stems, already

drooping in their fullness
at summer's end. Once

a lovely, balanced bed—seasons
of loss and patience
on public exhibition—

trampled by the clumsy
entrance of my Giantess.
I'm not home

and she knows it but somehow
found me at the cottage; it's

the porch

that is to blame, I'll wager,
wide and welcoming—
screened in, too, but torn
at nearly every seam

so bugs are finding me
delectable. *You'll break it*

I think to myself, all too aware
of her size, her chair. Her dress,
made of moth wings, impossibly

gathered, spills out, carpeting
the planks that make the floor.

She spends too long unfolding,
then refolding, rearranging—I see

there's fear in her
fidget, I fear
the wonder

has all drained, right from her center—

> not like honey from a hive,
> not like rain that pools, to overflow
> a loosened gutter—

> but like raisins
> in the fixed, essential grip
> of a toddler's fist—where

> chub, dirt, sweat, saliva mix
> with that one precious
> snack, until a new thing grabs

> their attention. Then, uncurling
> sticky digits, the old grapes fall

uneaten, forgotten altogether.

If they'd been seeds that fell,
(maybe sunflower)

a yellow kind of hope
could have arisen here

—which is simply untrue.
The porch is gray

entirely. Her hair is wiry, undone,
and Sorrow's overweight. I wait

for her to speak, fixing my vision
on barely-there-droplets-in-the-evening-air

—the water cycle, visible
but lacking

beauty, as I once imagined it.
How can I address her now,
regal yet unbecoming? I begin

with accusation.

www.ingramcontent.com/pod-product-compliance
Lightning Source LLC
Chambersburg PA
CBHW060417050426
42449CB00009B/2004